Cornerstones of Freedom

The Smithsonian Institution

MARY COLLINS

CHILDREN'S PRESS®
A Division of Grolier Publishing
New York • London • Hong Kong • Sydney
Danbury, Connecticut

Subject Consultant
Pamela M. Henson, Director
Institutional History Division
The Smithsonian Institution

Visit Children's Press on the Internet at:
http://publishing.grolier.com

Library of Congress Cataloging-in-Publication Data

Collins, Mary, 1961–
    The Smithsonian Institution / Mary Collins.
        p. cm.—(Cornerstones of freedom)
    Includes index.
    Summary: Describes the history of the Smithsonian Institution, its current
collections and challenges.
    ISBN: 0-516-21168-4 (lib. bdg.)   0-516-26518-0 (pbk.)
    1. Smithsonian Institution—History—Juvenile literature. [1. Smithsonian
Institution. 2. Museums.] I. Title. II. Series.
Q11.S8C64   1999
069'.09753—dc21

GROLIER
PUBLISHING

A Division of Grolier Publishing Co., Inc.
All rights reserved. Published simultaneously in Canada.
Printed in the United States of America.
1 2 3 4 5 6 7 8 9 10 R 08 07 06 05 04 03 02 01 00 99

Throughout history, only kings, queens, and other wealthy people could afford to collect and study unique works of art, or to own exotic animals from lands they had never visited. By the 1700s, things had changed, particularly in Europe, where people in both England and France built museums that displayed original art and historical objects for the educational benefit to all—rich and poor alike.

In 1800, the United States government, which had been based in Philadelphia, Pennsylvania, moved to its present-day location in Washington, D.C. One of the early buildings to be constructed was the Smithsonian Institution, a museum and research center dedicated to the collection and display of art, historical objects and documents, and to the exploration of the natural world. The sandstone "castle," however, wasn't really a castle. True to the democratic principles that lie at the root of our society, many people were allowed to view and work on the exhibits and collections, not just royalty. Since the Castle was completed in 1855, the Smithsonian has grown dramatically and now includes sixteen museums (nine of which are on the green lawn called the Mall that lies in front of the Castle), several research facilities where scientists study the galaxy and ecology, and the National Zoo.

In this aerial view of the Mall from the Washington Monument, the Capitol is at the opposite end and the Smithsonian Castle is the brown building on the right.

The National Air and Space Museum and the National Museum of Natural History remain two of the favorites. Since Air and Space opened in 1976, more than 175 million people have strolled under the remarkable collection of planes, space ships, and rockets on display in the lobby. A stuffed 8-ton male African elephant greets visitors as they enter the Natural History Museum. Indeed the Smithsonian collection has become so vast and varied, you never know what you'll find when you turn a corner. The Institution has a total of about 140 million objects, though only about 2 million are on display at any given time.

A British scientist, James Smithson, who never visited the United States, made all this possible when he left instructions in his will to provide

4

The elephant in the National Museum of Natural History stands more than 13 feet (4 meters) tall.

more than $500,000 to the U.S. government for the establishment of an institution devoted to the "increase and diffusion of knowledge." He died in 1829, when $500,000 was an even more astounding sum of money than it is today.

Smithson originally left his estate to his nephew, on the condition that if the nephew died childless, all of the money would go to the United States. When Smithson's nephew died in 1835, his relatives fought the transfer of the money. In 1838, a British court awarded the money to the United States. Later that year, Richard Rush, an American sent to London by President Andrew Jackson, accompanied 105 bags of gold coins across the Atlantic Ocean to the Philadelphia Mint.

James Smithson

James Polk

For eight years, the U.S. Congress argued over what to do with the money. Some congressmen wanted to create a National Library, others wanted to establish a National University. Finally, they agreed that in keeping with Smithson's interests they would establish a museum and research center for scientists. On August 10, 1846, President James Polk signed the bill that established the Smithsonian Institution.

No one knows why James Smithson left all of his money to Britain's former colonies. Since he had no children of his own, perhaps he felt the new nation would benefit the most from his estate. England and other European countries already had national museums, but not the United States. Smithson was a well-known scientist who studied gems and minerals. He understood the importance of education and the "diffusion of knowledge," especially for a young democracy.

Smithson's remains are buried in a chapel-like room near the north lobby of the Smithsonian Castle.

Once the United States had a national museum and research center, it had to decide what to do with it. What should be displayed? What should be studied? The first secretary (another word for president) of the Smithsonian, Joseph Henry, was a science professor at Princeton University in New Jersey and favored spending most of the Institution's money and time on creating a place where scientists could do their work. Not until Spencer Fullerton Baird took over as secretary in 1878 did the Smithsonian put more emphasis on its role as a museum with exhibits for

This statue of Joseph Henry outside the Smithsonian Castle overlooks the Mall.

everyone's enrichment. Baird was a naturalist who worked closely with John James Audubon, the famous illustrator who painted life-sized pictures of thousands of North American birds and animals. Baird wanted the Smithsonian to be a place that housed collections for the benefit of all people rather than an organization that financed the research of just a handful of scientists. Today, the Smithsonian manages to be both a place for scientific study and a place for the public to view and enjoy samples from the museums' holdings.

Spencer Fullerton Baird

The story of how the Smithsonian built its collections over the years is as interesting as the exhibits themselves. The 1800s were a time of great exploration both in the American West and around the world. The newly established Institution proved to be an ideal place to send items such as American-Indian headdresses or recently discovered plants. One of the first large collections donated to the Smithsonian came from the famous U.S. Exploring Expedition of 1838–42.

Led by the stern, disciplined, Lieutenant Charles Wilkes, a group of voyagers sailed around the world under orders from the U.S. government to find more seals for the fading seal industry. (Prior to electricity, seal fat was often burned in oil lamps for light.) They also were to map uncharted lands and to collect and study plants and animals. Lt. Wilkes had nine of the finest scientists of the day on board his ship. The disgruntled sailors who worked under extreme conditions—poor diet, constant exposure to the weather and sun, and a difficult commander—didn't

Lieutenant Charles Wilkes painted this portrait of the Vincennes, *the ship that carried the Exploring Expedition around the world.*

appreciate the researchers, who often wanted to be rowed ashore to study one thing or another. The sailors called the researchers "bug catchers." But those researchers made the four-year, 87,000-mile (140,000-kilometer) voyage a success.

They diagrammed hundreds of plants and animals that most people had never seen. They mapped miles of uncharted islands and shoreline, including 1,500 miles (2,400 km) of the Antarctic coastline at a time when most people thought there was either nothing there or a 3,000-mile (4,800-km)-wide hole! They followed the coastline of Oregon and saw the enormous Sitka Spruce for the first time. By journey's end, they had thousands of rare items to give to the newly established Smithsonian Institution, including an armadillo from off the tip of South America, a Hawaiian human-hair necklace, and gems, minerals, and rocks from the collections of the ship's famous geologist, James Dwight Dana.

The giant Diplodocus towers over the other dinosaur skeletons in the National Museum of Natural History.

Today, items from the U.S. Exploring Expedition represent just a tiny portion of the Smithsonian's amazing collections. At the National Museum of Natural History, you can walk by an 80-foot (24-meter)-long dinosaur called a *Diplodocus* and touch the jaws of a *Tyrannosaurus rex.* There is also a stuffed Indian tiger with 8-inch (20-centimeter)-wide paws that looks ready to pounce! There are plenty of people-related exhibits at this museum, too. Special re-creations called dioramas use life-sized mannequins to illustrate how cavemen might have lived or how an Arapaho Indian family from the Great Plains set up their tepee. Indeed the Natural History

The Indian tiger is a visitor favorite.

Museum is a mixture of all things found in the natural world—from fantastic rocks and fossils to insects and rare birds.

One of the other most popular museums, the National Air and Space Museum, has a more narrow focus but an equally dynamic collection. As you walk through the building, the enormous glass

The Wright brothers flew their plane for the first time on December 17, 1903, at Kitty Hawk, North Carolina.

ceiling rises up above you. Famous planes, space ships, and rockets hang in a dizzying array from cables. You can see the Wright Flyer, built and flown by Orville and Wilbur Wright, the first people ever to fly in a powered aircraft. Next to some of the more modern planes it looks like a fragile collection of wood and wire, but it worked! In other sections of the museum, you can look at different space suits and see how they have changed over the years. You can even step inside a lunar module and experience how it must have felt for the astronauts to work in such an incredibly small space while floating above Earth.

A visitor peers inside a lunar module.

The National Museum of American History sits just across the Mall from the Smithsonian's collection of spaceships. There are more earthly items there such as Kermit the Frog and Oscar the Grouch from *Sesame Street*. This museum focuses on objects that say something about our national character and culture. Included are dresses worn by First Ladies, old cars and trains, the ruby-red shoes that the actress Judy Garland wore when she played Dorothy in the movie, *The Wizard of Oz*, and the contents of a

First Lady Barbara Bush wore this gown at her husband George's Inaugural Ball on January 20, 1989.

A Smithsonian paleontologist works to get a fossil out of the surrounding rock.

simple wooden house that was lived in by a family that settled in the American West. Walking through the American History Museum makes it clear why many people call the Smithsonian "The Nation's Attic." Everything you could imagine is here. It's hard to believe that what visitors see accounts for only a tiny portion of the Institution's holdings.

Where are the rest of the holdings kept? Who decides what the Smithsonian takes in and what to display? Most of the Institution's items, such as the unusual egg collection, are stored in the museum buildings in areas where visitors aren't allowed to go. Many people work behind the scenes, such as a paleontologist, who might examine a fossil received from a scientist in Africa. Some of the bigger items, such as airplanes, are stored in warehouses around the Washington area.

Despite the number of items in the Smithsonian's collection, the Institution is highly selective about objects that are accepted. Curators, people who organize and study museum collections, cannot possibly take in everything they receive. No artifact or specimen is accepted unless it is approved by a committee of curators. Many things are sent anonymously, which means no one knows who sent them. (Dorothy's red shoes from *The Wizard of Oz* are an example.) Some people, such as James Dwight Dana, the geologist who traveled on the Exploring Expedition, donate their findings.

The Smithsonian has its own staff of scientists who are sent into the field to collect specimens. Dr. Terry Irwin, who studies beetles from all

The Insect Zoo contains an extensive collection of fascinating specimens from all over the world.

Insects won't inherit the earth— they own it now.

Thomas Eisner, Entomologist

ORKIN
INSECT
ZOO

The Amazing Arthropods

 over the world, has added more than one thousand new species to the museum's collection. Another Smithsonian entomologist (a person who studies insects), Dr. Beth Norden, travels across the world in search of stinging bugs. Since many of her specimens are sensitive to changes in temperature and air pressure she can't always pack them in her luggage when she boards an airplane. Usually she tries to keep them with her in small bottles, but on one occasion she carried large, live grasshoppers in her purse!

True to the vision of the Smithsonian's first secretary, Joseph Henry, many of the scientists at the Smithsonian not only add to collections, but they conduct important research that furthers the understanding of all scientists in their fields. At the Conservation and Research Center in Front Royal, Virginia, staffers work to improve the birth and survival rate of endangered animals. The Smithsonian's Astrophysical Observatory is based in Cambridge, Massachusetts. At observatories in Arizona and Hawaii, astronomers study the universe through powerful telescopes. The Institution even has a research facility in Panama, where scientists study native cultures and the evolution and behavior of tropical animals and plants.

The general public rarely sees what goes on at the research centers, which cater to professional scientists. But each time visitors stop at an exhibit they get to see the handiwork of other staffers at the Smithsonian. The 80-foot (24-m) *Diplodocus* in the Natural History Museum took more than a year to get out of the rock in Utah where it was found. Then, once it was shipped to the Smithsonian, it took the museum staff seven years to put all the pieces together and to mount the final skeleton.

Conservators, people who are in charge of preserving and cleaning all of the objects in the collections, worry about how light, dust, and air might affect an item. Fabrics, such as those in the collection of First Ladies' gowns, are especially vulnerable to decay. When staffers decided to refurbish the dress President James Garfield's wife, Lucretia, wore to his Inaugural Ball in 1881, they found that even though it looks white today people who attended the ball described the color as "delicate lavender." After some careful research and a more thorough look at the gown, conservators concluded that indeed Mrs. Garfield's dress had been colored with a light-sensitive purple dye. The bright bulbs that allowed visitors to see it more clearly had caused the color to fade.

Lucretia Garfield's gown now is kept in a dimly lit exhibit to protect the delicate fabric from further damage.

The popular gem, mineral, and rock exhibit, also located in the Natural History Museum, required the skill of more than two hundred people. Curators had to pick out the best samples for each display, then designers had to decide the best way to show them off. Writers had to pen the small paragraphs that accompany each portion of the exhibit, as well as the pamphlets the museum staffers hand out to visitors. A Hollywood specialist in making movie sets created a make-believe mine shaft so visitors can experience what work conditions are like

There are many people who work behind the scenes to make Smithsonian displays, such as this topaz exhibit, interesting and informative.

for miners. Dozens of people from a security company put together the sealed case that holds one of the world's largest and most-famous jewels, the Hope Diamond. The 45-carat blue gem sits at the center of the exhibit in a clear box with a rotating center. The light shimmers off its sharp edges each time it turns.

The Hope Diamond is one of the most-photographed exhibits at the Smithsonian.

This visitor is using a virtual reality display featuring a Space Shuttle.

A walk through any of the museums involves all of your senses. Nearly every main exhibit includes a short movie, some kind of interactive computer screen, actual objects that you can touch and smell, and a story written on the wall. At the U.S. Postal Museum, a three-dimensional character follows you through a section of the exhibit, explaining how the United States mail system got started and how it works today. Visit the Hands-On History room at the Museum of

American History and try to guess the function of the objects in one of the boxes on the shelf. Some were everyday items during life in the 1800s, but are unrecognizable today. For those who tire of being indoors, try the Hirshhorn Museum's outdoor sculpture garden, which has life-sized statues.

Visitors stroll through the Hirshhorn Sculpture Garden.

During the summer months, visitors can enjoy not only the regular exhibits but also the Smithsonian's famous outdoor Folk Festival. Each year the Institution picks a theme— "Native American Cultures," for example, or "The American South"—and brings in musicians, craftspeople, speakers, singers, and sometimes even animals for a two-week celebration that is also an education. You can even take a spin on the Smithsonian's old-fashioned merry-go-round.

For those who never make it to Washington, look for the Smithsonian's traveling exhibits, which visit cities both large and small across the United States. As part of its 150th anniversary

Visitors enjoy a display of musical instruments at a recent Smithsonian Folk Festival.

celebration tour in 1996–97, the Smithsonian's display went to many U.S. states. Dorothy's ruby-red shoes from *The Wizard of Oz* were just one of the many popular items in that show.

A favorite display for visitors is the flag that inspired Francis Scott Key to write "The Star-Spangled Banner" during the War of 1812. Key's poem was later set to music and became the United States's national anthem. (The flag, currently under renovation, is displayed at the National Museum of American History.)

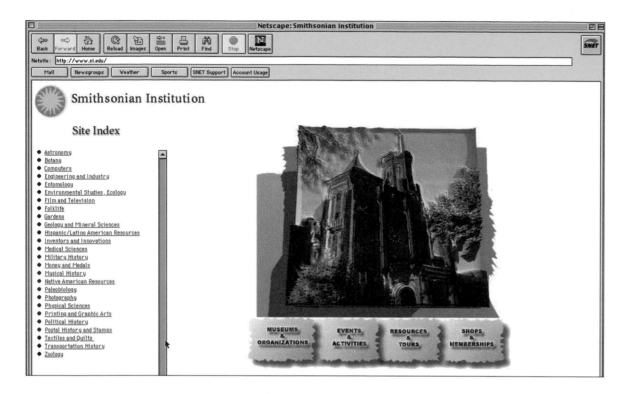

Netscape: Smithsonian Institution

Netsite: http://www.si.edu/

Mail | Newsgroups | Weather | Sports | SNET Support | Account Usage

Smithsonian Institution

Site Index

- Astronomy
- Botany
- Computers
- Engineering and Industry
- Entomology
- Environmental Studies, Ecology
- Film and Television
- Folklife
- Gardens
- Geology and Mineral Sciences
- Hispanic/Latino American Resources
- Inventors and Innovations
- Medical Sciences
- Military History
- Money and Medals
- Musical History
- Native American Resources
- Paleobiology
- Photography
- Physical Sciences
- Printing and Graphic Arts
- Political History
- Postal History and Stamps
- Textiles and Quilts
- Transportation History
- Zoology

MUSEUMS & ORGANIZATIONS | EVENTS & ACTIVITIES | RESOURCES & TOURS | SHOPS & MEMBERSHIPS

The Smithsonian Institution website offers a chance to visit the museums without traveling to Washington, D.C.

Another way to visit the Smithsonian without going to Washington is through the Internet. The Smithsonian maintains an extensive website at *www.si.edu* where online visitors can see virtual exhibits, learn about Smithsonian history, take a tour of the museum in 1886, and learn about the work done behind the scenes at the Smithsonian.

The most remarkable thing about the Smithsonian Institution remains that anyone can visit the exhibits for free. They are there, just as James Smithson wanted them to be, for the educational benefit of the general population. The Institution has added computers and videos, restaurants, and gift shops that cater to the millions of visitors that come each year from around the world. But it's the simplest objects on display that will hold your imagination.

Pick up the Stone Age ax that sits in one of the boxes in the Discovery Room in the Natural History Museum. Feel what it must have been like for one of our ancestors to hold that same tool about 100,000 years ago in a place now called Libya. That is what Smithson meant when he talked about "the diffusion of knowledge." The Smithsonian Institution is here today to honor that vision.

Anyone who visits the Discovery Room at the Natural History Museum can hold the Stone Age ax.

25

A LISTING AND DESCRIPTION OF ALL

IN WASHINGTON, D.C.

Anacostia Museum
1901 Fort Place, SE

Originally a neighborhood center, this museum highlights the African-American experience, particularly in the South.

Arthur M. Sackler Gallery
1050 Independence Avenue, SW

A unique mixture of work from ancient and living Asian artists.

Arts and Industries Building
900 Jefferson Drive, SW (next to the Smithsonian Castle)

This building was erected in 1881 to be the first National Museum. It housed the natural history, art, anthropology, and history collections. The Arts and Industries Building now houses exhibits for the African American Museum Project and a Science on the Mall gallery will open in 2000.

Freer Gallery of Art
Jefferson Drive at 12th Street, SW

One of the world's finest collections of Asian art, including work from China, Korea, and Japan, as well as a large collection of works by Whistler.

Hirshhorn Museum and Sculpture Garden
Independence Avenue at 7th Street, SW

The sunken gardens hide a wonderful collection of sculptures, but don't forget to go inside and see some of the modern paintings.

National Air and Space Museum
Independence Avenue at 6th Street, SW

This museum tells the story of the history of flight and space travel. The Samuel P. Langley Theater has an enormous screen that shows films on flight and the environment (including an up-close-and-personal look at a volcano). Also check out the stars at the Albert Einstein Planetarium.

National Museum of African Art
950 Independence Avenue, SW

Collections and traditional arts from Africa south of the Sahara Desert.

National Museum of American Art
8th and G Streets, NW

This museum showcases American painting, sculpture, photography, and folk art from the 1700s to the present. Be sure to look at some of the early paintings of the American West. They were the "photographs" of their time and profoundly influenced how Americans in the East saw the West.

National Museum of American History
Constitution Avenue between 12th and 14th Streets, NW

The odd collection of objects that were originally held in the U.S. Patent Office under the official title of "The National Cabinet of Curiosities" became the start of the National Museum of American History in 1858. This museum remains a peculiar mixture of household items and Americana even today. See everything from First

Ladies' dresses to the plain dishes used by a Western farm family. Be sure to visit the Hands-On Science Center on the first floor and the Hands-On History Center on the second floor.

National Museum of Natural History/National Museum of Man
Constitution Avenue at 10th Street, NW

Visit here to get a better understanding of the natural world and people's place in it. A six-story Discovery Center in the West Wing includes a Hands-On Science room for kids and a movie theater.

National Portrait Gallery
8th and F Streets, NW

This is one of only a handful of museums in the world that is devoted to portraits. Here visitors will find portraits of some of the most important people in American history—from Abraham Lincoln to Dr. Martin Luther King Jr. The portraits come in all sizes and formats, including life-sized statues, photographs, and oil paintings.

National Postal Museum
2 Massachusetts Avenue, at First Street, NE (across from Union Station)

Learn the fascinating history of how Americans have received their mail over the years.

National Zoological Park
Connecticut Avenue, 3000 block

See page 28.

Renwick Gallery of the National Museum of American Art
Pennsylvania Avenue at 17th Street, NW

This gallery became part of the Smithsonian in 1972 and displays items from American craft artists, such as quilts, fine wooden bowls, and handmade furniture.

IN NEW YORK CITY

Cooper-Hewitt National Design Museum
2 East 91st Street

Who designed the paper cup or the paper clip? You can find out the origins of some of the most common items in our world today at this unique museum.

National Museum of the American Indian
George Gustav Heye Center
Alexander Hamilton Custom House
One Bowling Green
(A new building for this museum is scheduled to open on the Mall in Washington, D.C., around 2002.)

A look at the history of American Indians from their arrival thousands of years ago to their life on reservations today.

THE NATIONAL ZOO

This photograph, taken around 1885, shows two of the buffalo that roamed in the yard behind the Smithsonian Castle.

When you think of a museum, you might not think about live animals, but the Smithsonian does have a zoo. From the Institution's beginnings, people donated creatures to the Smithsonian. At one point, there were six buffalo on the Mall behind the Castle and many other odd species housed inside! In 1889, Congress created a better

home for these animals when it established the National Zoological Park on a large piece of wooded land that runs along a stream called Rock Creek in Washington, D.C. Today 5,500 animals live there, making it one of the largest and most famous zoos in the world.

In recent years, the zoo has been transformed from a place where animals huddle in empty cages to a lush, natural habitat where each species lives in an exhibit that closely matches its natural setting in the wild. When you visit Amazonia, the newest of the eighteen major exhibits, you'll walk into a steamy rain forest complete with a stream and birds overhead. The lizards and other animals roam free so watch where you step!

An orangutan swings along the O-line high above the National Zoo.

Outside you'll notice a series of silver towers strung with cables that make up The Orangutan Transport System (O-line). Here, orangutans love to swing over visitors' heads as the people shuttle between the Ape House and a place called the Think Tank. It seems that the orangutans enjoy watching the visitors as much as the visitors enjoy watching them!

GLOSSARY

Americana – objects that seem uniquely American, such as Kermit the Frog

array – a large number of things

authentic – real or genuine

carat – a weight measurement for precious stones

designer – person who decides how to position the objects in a museum exhibit and how to light the exhibit area for best effect

diffusion – the spreading of information to others through contact and experience

diorama – museum exhibit that re-creates in great detail a setting that involves people in another place and time

geologist – scientist who studies rocks

Mall – the green lawn that lies between the Lincoln Memorial and the Capitol in Washington, D.C.

mint – place where coins are manufactured

naturalist – person who studies animals and plants

unique – unlike anything else

paleontologist – scientist who studies fossils to learn more about life on Earth before humans

principle – basic truth, law, or belief

refurbish – to fix up something that has begun to fade or fall apart

Stone Age – period in history when stone was commonly used to make tools and weapons; different parts of the world experienced a Stone Age at different times

will – written instructions stating what should happen to someone's property and money when a person dies

The Hope Diamond is 45 carats.

paleontologist

TIMELINE

James Smithson born in France	**1765**
Smithson dies; wills estate to nephew	**1829**
Smithson's nephew dies	**1835**
Richard Rush escorts money to Philadelphia	**1838**
	1846 *August 10:* President James Polk signs bill creating Smithsonian Institution
Joseph Henry serves as first secretary	**1855** The Castle is built
	1878
Spencer Fullerton Baird serves as secretary	**1881** Arts and Industries Building opens as first National Museum Building
	1887
Congress establishes National Zoo	**1889**
National Museum of American Art collection is created	**1906**
	1910 Natural History Museum opens
	1923 Freer Gallery of Art opens
	1946 National Air Museum is created
	1962 National Portrait Gallery opens
	1964 Museum of History and Technology opens; name later changed to National Museum of American History
Hirshhorn Museum and Sculpture Garden opens	**1974**
	1976 New National Air and Space Museum building opens
	1996 The 150th anniversary of the Smithsonian
	1999 Discovery Center at the National Museum of Natural History opens
Scheduled completion date for the National Museum of the American Indian	**2002**

INDEX *(**Boldface** page numbers indicate illustrations.)*

PHOTO CREDITS

©: Andrew H. Macdonald: cover, 4, 5 top, 10 top, 11 top, 14, 15, 18, 25, 26, 27; Art Resource, NY: 5 bottom, 7 bottom, 31 top (National Portrait Gallery, Smithsonian Institution); Jay Mallin: 13, 16, 19, 20, 23, 30; Mae Scanlan: 2, 6 bottom, 7 top, 10 bottom, 11 bottom, 12, 17, 21, 29, 31 bottom; Peabody Essex Museum, Salem, MA.: 9; Smithsonian Institution, Washington, DC.: 22 (Richard W. Strauss), 8, 24, 28; Stock Montage, Inc.: 6 top; Tony Stone Images: 1 (Jon Ortner).

ABOUT THE AUTHOR

Mary Collins works as a special project editor for National Geographic *World* magazine. She also freelances for a variety of national publications and is the author of several Children's Press books, including *The Spanish-American War* and *Mount Vernon* (Cornerstones of Freedom). She lives in Alexandria, Virginia.